SLIME

Kitchen Experiment

By Meg Gaertner

Published by The Child's World®
1980 Lookout Drive • Mankato, MN 56003-1705
800-599-READ • www.childsworld.com

Photographs ©: Rick Orndorf, cover, 1, 14, 16, 17, 18, 19, 20,
21; iStockphoto, 5, 9; Vystek Images/Shutterstock Images, 6;
Nadia Leskovskaya/Shutterstock Images, 11; Thanthima Lim/
Shutterstock Images, 12; Shutterstock Images, 13

ISBN 9781503825338
LCCN 2017959696

Printed in the United States of America
PA02378

Table of Contents

CHAPTER 1

What's the Matter?

Matter is anything that takes up space. Everything around us is matter! **Mass** is the amount of matter in an object. All matter has mass.

There are different states, or types, of matter. **Solids** have their own shape. This shape stays the same. A chair or a blanket is a solid.

Liquids can change their shape. They move and flow. They are also wet.

These blocks are made of wood. Wood is a solid.

Milk is a liquid.
It can be poured
into a glass.

Water and milk are liquids. Liquids take the shape of what they are in.

Gases are all around us. We cannot always see them. We breathe air, which is a gas. Gases change even more than liquids. A gas will spread out and fill any shape. When we blow up a balloon, we fill it with gas.

Sometimes matter changes from one state to another. Water can be in any state of matter. We drink water as a liquid. When water is very cold, it becomes ice. Ice is water as a solid. If we heat water, it becomes steam. Steam is water as a gas.

TIP

The name "oobleck" comes from a Dr. Seuss book, *Bartholomew and the Oobleck!*

We will learn how to make **slime** in the kitchen. Slime is something wet and slippery like mud. Is slime a solid or a liquid? The slime we will make is called oobleck. Oobleck is made with cornstarch and water. It can act like a liquid *and* like a solid.

Slime can be any color.

CHAPTER 2

Here's the Solution!

We will make slime by mixing things together. The slime will be a **solution**. A solution is a solid **dissolved** in a liquid. A solid dissolves when it looks like it fades away. For example, when we add sugar to lemonade, the sugar dissolves. We can't see the sugar. But if we drink the lemonade, it tastes sweet. The sugar is still in the solution.

Lemonade is made with lemons, water, and sugar.

A solution has two parts. The **solvent** is the liquid part. It makes other things dissolve. We will use water as our solvent.

Cornstarch is made from field corn. Animals such as cows eat field corn.

The **solute** is the solid part. It dissolves into the liquid. We will use cornstarch as our solute. Together the water and cornstarch will make our slime solution.

Honey is a thick liquid. It is also very sticky.

Solutions can be thick or thin. Honey is thick. It flows slowly. Fruit juice is thin. It flows quickly. Adding more solvent makes a solution thinner. Adding more solute makes a solution thicker.

CHAPTER 3

THE EXPERIMENT
Let's Get Slimed!

MATERIALS LIST

mixing bowl
1 cup (237 mL) water
food coloring
1.5 cups (192 g) corn starch

TIME TO FINISH: 10–15 minutes

TIP
All of the supplies are safe. But it is not a good idea to eat this slime. It won't taste very good!

1. Pour the water into the mixing bowl.

2. Add a few drops of food coloring to the water. Add more drops for more color.

TIP
When the slime is smooth, the cornstarch has dissolved into the water.

3. Add the cornstarch to the mixing bowl.

Use your hands to mix the solution.

Keep mixing until it is smooth. The slime is smooth when it looks the same all over.

4. Try forming a ball of slime in your hands. If you can't, add a little more cornstarch. This makes the solution thicker. Mix it in until you can form a ball. The slime has become more like a solid.

5. Try holding the slime in your hands. It should drip like a liquid. If it does not, add a little more water. This makes the solution thinner.

6. When you are finished playing with the slime, you can keep it in a plastic zip bag. Add water the next time you want to play with it.

TIP
Use warm water to clean the slime off your hands and clothes.

Glossary

dissolved (di-ZOLVD) A solid has dissolved when it seems to fade into a liquid. Sugar can be dissolved in water.

gases (GASS-es) Gases are types of matter that fill any space they are in. The air we breathe is made of several gases.

liquids (LIK-wids) Liquids are types of matter that can fill containers. Water and milk are liquids.

mass (MASS) Mass is how much matter an object has. All objects have mass.

matter (MAT-ur) Matter is anything that takes up space. Matter also has mass.

slime (SLIME) Slime is something wet and slippery. Slime can be made with cornstarch and water.

solids (SOL-ids) Solids are types of matter that do not change their shapes. Chairs and tables are solids.

solute (SOL-yoot) A solute is the solid part of a solution. A solute can be dissolved in a liquid.

solution (suh-LOO-shuhn) A solution is a mix of a solid and a liquid. Slime is a solution.

solvent (SOL-vuhnt) A solvent is the liquid part of a solution. A solid is dissolved into the solvent.

To Learn More

In the Library

Lawrence, Ellen. *Liquids and Solids*. New York, NY: Bearport, 2015.

Montgomery, Anne. *Solid or Liquid?* Huntington Beach, CA: Teacher Created Materials, 2015.

Reilly, Kathleen M. *Explore Solids and Liquids!* White River Junction, VT: Nomad Press, 2014.

On the Web

Visit our Web site for links about slime:
childsworld.com/links

Note to Parents, Teachers, and Librarians: We routinely verify our Web links to make sure they are safe and active sites. So encourage your readers to check them out!

Index

About the Author

Meg Gaertner is a children's book author and editor who lives in Minnesota. When not writing, she enjoys dancing and spending time outdoors.